The

Quick & Dirty Guide Series

Publishing advice from a self-published author

Samantha Warren

A Note From the Author

As a self-published author, I have written and published over 15 novels and novellas and countless short stories. I have made a decent amount of money and done massive amounts of research into self-publishing. I have made mistakes and learned from them. Why tell you this? Because unlike a lot of how-to guide authors out there, I have been in the trenches of self-publishing. I have done the work. I have had the learning curve. My techniques come from personal experience, not just theory. I am here to share with you what I have learned in my years in the self-publishing world, so you can break from the gate with speed and grace. Unlike me, who stumbled and faltered. I'm here to help you navigate the waters of self-publishing, so pick up that paddle and let's get rowing!

Table of Contents

Self-Editing

Why do we need to edit?

A quick note: This book is not meant to be a comprehensive explanation of all the grammar rules that exist in the insanely complicated English language. This is simply meant to share the process I use and to help you get through the editing process. For help with the grammar part of editing, check out Strunk & White's The Elements of Style *or Jessica Bell's* Polish Your Fiction. *While I do my best to be grammatically correct, I've been known to ignore acceptable conventions simply because I don't like them. Like that whole split infinitive thing? I LOVE splitting my infinitives, no matter how many times I've been told to not do it, I just can't help myself. They beg to be split!*

So you've just dumped gallons of blood onto the page and now you finally have a completed book. Congratulations! Sit back, have a glass of wine, make someone take you for a celebratory dinner. Get a good night's sleep. Because tomorrow, tomorrow you'll be back at it, hacking away at that lovely little baby you just created with a scalpel, and maybe a chainsaw.

Some people hate editing. Some people love it. I'm one of those weird folks who prefers the editing part to the writing. I love going back through what I've written like a plastic surgeon with a patient, making my book just that much more beautiful. (I'll also admit, I generally like reading through my books again. I only write stuff I like reading, and editing gives me a chance to realize that what felt like drivel while I was writing really isn't so bad.)

Some people suggest you put your book in a drawer for three months and forget about it. If you have the time to do that, great. Go for it. That doesn't work for me. I usually take a day or two away from the book, read, watch television, start something else, whatever. But then I'm back at it, plugging away to get the book finished. Either way, you're going to need to edit it at some point.

Editing is *super important*. You *have* to do it. Okay, so you don't *have* to. No one is going to come to your house and lock you in the shower with 1000 bees if you don't... eh, no promises there. They might. More likely, though, is you'll publish your book and get a slew of 1-star ratings for producing what is fondly referred to in the publishing world as "crap". You don't want to produce crap or you wouldn't be reading this book. So I'm going to take you through the process I've developed over the years to help you edit the work you just created. Ready? Good. Let's get started.

Make a Timeline

Before you start editing, take the time to make a *timeline*. Knowing what happens when is extremely helpful when you're reading through your book. It can be as simple or complex as you want it to be. I generally do mine by hand on a sheet of paper, in pencil. I'll inevitably want to change things on the timeline as I'm reading through. But having that timeline before you begin editing will save you some time and headache trying to figure out where things are supposed to go.

A *scene list* is also useful. If you use Scrivener, like I do, you probably already have one in your chapter/scene titles. A scene list is similar to the timeline, but slightly more detailed. Both will help you keep on track as you edit.

Okay. Now we're really ready to edit. Onto the fun!

The Pen & Paper Step

After I have my timeline, I use Scrivener to compile my book into a mobi so I can put it on my Kindle. If you don't have Scrivener, you can just email the document to your Kindle or load it onto whatever e-reader you use. If you don't have an e-reader*, you can print it off or read it directly on the computer. I advise against reading it on the computer if you can avoid it, though. That switch in format helps a lot. We'll use a similar method later on in the process, too, but for now, you have your completely raw, unedited book somewhere that you can read it.

Now grab a notebook and a pen or pencil. I like pencils, but that's just me. Get yourself a cup of tea/coffee/wine, plop yourself in a comfortable chair, and get ready to read.

Read through your book, paying specific attention to anything that seems off to you. Note the chapter/scene on your paper along with any thoughts that pop into your head about fixing it. Don't worry about spelling issues, typos, etc. You're looking at the story right now, not proofing the book. Make notes about *anything* that require changes. Any wrong character names, plot lines that disappear, scenes that don't work, that kind of stuff. Write down everything, big and small. This is your time to catch those content issues that will steal your stars when it comes time for reviews. Trust me, the readers will see them, so if you see them and choose to ignore them, they will call you out on it. Guaranteed.

Spend the time now before you publish, read through thoroughly, and find the sticking points. Once you have your notebook filled with problem points and have killed off three pens, you're ready for step three.

Note: I highly suggest you buy an e-reader of some sort if you're going to be publishing a lot of books. You need to be able to read in the same format your readers are going to be using, and it will be just that much more difficult to check for errors if you don't have an actual e-reader. Consider it a business expense.

Big Changes First

This really should be a no-brainer, but for some reason, I didn't think about it until I read Rachel Aaron's *2k to 10k: Writing Faster, Writing Better, and Writing More of What You Love*. She mentioned one simple, obvious thing, and it completely changed the way I edit.

Change the big stuff first. I used to edit chronologically, from beginning to end. I'd start at Chapter 1 and work my way through. Then, of course, by the time I got to the end, I'd have to go back and fix things at the beginning again that changed halfway through. Crazy, right?

Now I work smarter, not harder. Deal with the big stuff first. Look through the list of fixes that are needed and figure out which ones are going to cause the biggest changes to your work. Is there an extraneous character that you need to take out completely? Do that first. Make the big changes early on so you're not doing twice the work later.

Once you have all the big changes done, work your way through the list in order of importance. Leave the small, piddly stuff for the end. After you've done the big stuff, the little stuff will be super easy and you'll be able to knock them out in no time at all.

Proofread
"Read as a reader"

After all those big, ginormous changes are made, it's time to do the first proofread. Yes, I said 'first'. The next three steps are all forms of proofreading, and they're all important.

Before I start my proofread, I run spellcheck on whatever program I'm using. I actually generally do it twice because that's the way I roll. Why do all the work myself when I can outsource to the computer, right?

When I've finished with that, I'll export to a mobi again and load it back onto my Kindle. You can print it or load it onto your e-reader or whatever method you choose, just like before. However, a little caveat: At this stage, I really really really (add a few more reallys in here) recommend *not* using the computer. Changing your reading format is very helpful in catching the small issues like typos. I don't know why. It just is.

So curl up in your chair with your e-reader or printed copy and start reading. If you have an e-reader, you should be able to highlight any issues. I prefer my Kindle Fire because I can highlight with several colors. If you're using paper, you can mark the tricky spots with a pen.

The main goal on this read-through is to note anything that draws the reader (you) out of the reading experience. That is the main thing we do not want to do. The reading experience is everything and we want to keep it as seamless as possible. This is essentially a slightly more detailed proofread. I often will make note of any sentences that are awkward or other things that need changing.

Then, obviously, once you're done, you're going to make those changes.

Get Fresh Eyes

This next step in the process is super duper uper important. Yes, I said uper. Deal with it. You need to get a fresh set of eyes. There are seven billion other people out there who can look at your book for you. Find one or two of them and pass that thing off. It's extremely helpful if you can afford a professional edit at this point. Or at least a professional proofreader. Freelancers who used to be in traditional publishing are all over the place at varying rates, and if you can get your hands on one of them, superb. If not, give your book to a Grammar Nazi friend or family member. Find someone with an eye for detail. Hunt down that person who is always correcting your posts on Facebook. Hop on Fiverr and hire one of those guys.

Get your book to someone else. You've been staring at it for too long and your mind is now trained to skip over the mistakes. You need the outside input to help you stay focused.

Another Caveat: You will still have mistakes. Books are like people. None are perfect. Here's a little anecdote from my past publishing experience:

When I wrote my paranormal romance, I hired two editors and sent the book to seven beta readers. That's ten people, counting me. I sent it out for reviews and hit publish. The very first reviewer contacted me in an email. "Uh, did you know you kept saying ephemeral when you meant ethereal?" Color me embarrassed. Thank goodness ebooks let you make changes so quickly. I fixed it and uploaded the new version. Then I started writing my next book.

The moral of the story is: *Nothing is perfect, and that's okay. Do your best, correct your mistakes, and move on.*

Listen to the Audio

This last step is super helpful, but it's one I often neglect. My resolution for this year is to use this method of proofreading on every single book I produce.

So how do you do it?

Simple. Listen to your book. Plug in your headphones, set your book to text-to-talk, and just listen. Most e-readers will do this nowadays, but if you don't have an e-reader, you can use your computer. You'll want to follow along as you listen so you know what the story is actually supposed to say. Our minds tend to fill in mistakes, especially after we've read them so many times. These last two steps, *Getting Fresh Eyes* and *Listen to the Audio,* are designed to help overcome the faults of your own mind and produce the best book you possibly can. As a self-publisher, you don't want to be responsible for adding to the poor opinion many people have of us. *Produce quality work to achieve quality results.*

And now that you're done editing, it's time to **PARTY!**

Seriously. Go out, have some fun, and congratulate yourself on truly completing your book. Enjoy the feeling. Get up in the morning and publish that baby so the world can share in your creativity.

Then you get to start the whole process over again! How exciting! Being a writer is awesome, but one thing's for sure: you'll never be quite finished. One story idea will lead to another, and then another, then another. You'll have a notebook full of ideas you'll never have time to finish. It's a vicious cycle that we all get sucked into, but we wouldn't have it any other way.

Happy writing!

Ebook
Formatting

First Thing's First

So let's get down to it. First thing's first. *Your book must be edited.* This is not an option. Do it yourself (Quick & Dirty Self-Editing coming soon), hire a professional editor, or beg and plead with one of your grammar Nazi friends to do it, but get it done. (By the way, I highly recommend options #2 and #3 over #1.) Let me repeat:

Edit your book.

Don't just write it and throw it up for the world to see. Don't publish crap. The self-publishing gods will hunt you down and put slivers under your toenails if you do. Say it with me: *I must edit my book. I must edit my book. I must edit my book.*

Okay, good. So now that we've gone through that, on to step #2:

Get a professional cover.

"Don't judge a book by its cover" only applies to people. I can guarantee that if you put up a crappy cover, people will absolutely judge it for you. A good, eye-catching cover is the easiest way to get people to look at your book, so get a good cover.

To recap what we've learned so far:
-Edit
-Get a good cover

Now we can get down to the nitty gritty and focus on why you really bought this book.

Formatting a simple fiction Ebook

There are a few ways to go about formatting an ebook. If you have a program like Scrivener, it will do a lot for you. However, you shouldn't trust a program to do all your formatting for you. Make sure you double-check everything before you hit Publish. You can also use programs like Calibre to turn a file into a mobi, ePub, etc. The method I use is quick, easy, and produces a nice file. I use OpenOffice and a .doc file, which is generally accepted anywhere you go. Word will work just the same if you have that handy, though some of the menus might be slightly different.

Step 1: Formatting the body

Before I mess with the chapter titles or anything else, I do a CTRL+A --> Format --> Paragraph.

Under **Indents & Spacing**, everything should be set to 0.00", except **First Line**. I set that to 0.25", which gives the paragraphs a nice indent without being glaringly annoying. Do *not* use automatic. I don't mess with any spaces above and below the paragraphs as people can change stuff like that on their ereaders if they want spaces between the lines. **Line Spacing** should be set to Single. Anything else may cause issues with certain eretailer sites.

Under **Alignment**, I set **Options** to **Left**. Ereaders generally justify the text on their own when they convert the files, but if you're going to be producing a PDF, you can choose *Justified* here instead.

While everything is highlighted, this is also the time you'll want to choose your font and font size. I generally go with Times New Roman and size 12. Again, the reader can pick their own font and size on their ereader, so it's best to keep this part generic.

Step 2: Title Page

Most ebook distributors will add a cover to the file automatically, so I don't bother adding those. The very first thing I add is my title page. What do you include?

-Title (and series if applicable)
-Author
-All Rights Reserved.
-Copyright Info
Feel free to copy my title page and change it to suit your needs.

Fun Fact: To get the copyright symbol on a PC, hold ALT and press 0169 on your number pad. On a Mac, it's Option+G.

Step 3: Chapter Titles

Depending on which book I'm writing, I treat chapter titles differently. On my *Jane* series of vampire novellas, I write out the number and surround it by pretty little crosses that fit the feel of the book.

ONE

For my paranormal romance, *The Iron Locket*, I use something more magical.

ONE

With my zombie western, *Massacre at Lonesome Ridge,* I went plain and simple.

Chapter 1

Whatever you choose to do, be consistent and make sure it looks good on an ereader. Some of those fancy characters don't show up with certain fonts or look terrible, and ereaders can only read a handful of fonts. Double-check anything you do before you publish.

Now that you've figured out how you want your chapter titles to look, let's make them look good. Highlight your chapter title. Either do a CTRL+B or click the little B in the edit bar at the top. Change the font size to 14. Next, *right click* and choose Paragraph. Under Indents & Spacing, set everything to 0.00". Under Alignment, choose Center. Then press Okay. Do this for every chapter title and scene break (those places where you use ***).

Note: If you're comfortable with OpenOffice or Word, you can set up Styles to do this for you. Personally, I don't like using them. When I did, I would get files rejected from places like Smashwords before they put strange things in the file that shouldn't be there. Doing it by hand is only slightly more time consuming and I know it's going to look the way I want it to look.

Step 4: End Matter

The end matter is the last thing your reader will see. I like to include three things:

A thank you page with a link to my email list
A list of other books I've written
My bio/contact page

Email List Sign-up

If you don't already have an email list, you should create one ASAP. Email lists are the best way to keep in touch with readers and you don't have to worry about places like Facebook and Twitter closing down. On the sign-up page, thank the reader for reading your book and provide the link to your email list. It helps to offer something of value to them, such as updates, a free story, or other fun things. On this same page, you can also include a direct link to the next book in the series (only if this is your Amazon file. Smashwords will not accept the book if it includes a link like that.)

Other Books

On my other books list, I include all the other books I have written. Now that my list is getting a bit large, I include the series titles instead of the actual books.

Bio/Contact Page

This page is crucial. When a reader likes your book, they'll often want to know more about you and how to contact you. On this page, you need a short bio, an email address, and a link to your Facebook and Twitter pages.

And that's it. Your book is formatted!

A Note on Adding Images

Some people like to add images to their books. That's great and adds a bit of visual interest, but there are a couple things to keep in mind.

- Keep the images small. Large images will cause the reading experience to slow down. They could even cause some ereaders to crash.
- Keep the images grayscale. While some ereaders can deal with color, most can't yet. Also, color images are generally larger.
- Keep the cost of delivery in mind. Many eretailers will charge you to deliver your book. When it's just text, those costs are minimal, but as you add images, the delivery charges grow. You don't want to lose all your profit because your images were too big.

Table of Contents

Most fiction books don't really need a table of contents. People are not generally going to be skipping around through the chapters and since ereaders hold your place, they won't need to know what page they're on. But if you'd like to add a table of contents for some reason, the easiest way is using Bookmarks. You'll bookmark a spot in your file, then add a link to that on your table of contents.

Publishing Your Formatted Ebook

Now that your book is all pretty and stuff, publishing it is super easy. You'll want to create accounts in a minimum of two places. Amazon and Smashwords.

Who are the power players?

-Amazon: Amazon is the major retailer. They came into the game with the Kindle and continue to hold the market's share of ebooks. Some people may choose to just go through Amazon to use KDP Select, but as the saying goes, don't put all your eggs in one basket.

-Barnes & Noble: B&N with their Nook still has a big catalog, even though they're slowly slipping toward the bottom.

-Kobo: Kobo is fairly new to the game, but they're quickly picking up steam.

-iTunes: iTunes is steadily growing in the ebook market, even despite that little gaff they had with the law. You need a Mac to go direct to iTunes. I don't have a Mac, ergo I use....

-Smashwords: SW is a distributor who will take your ebook and send it to every eretailer but Amazon.

-Draft2Digital: Smashwords's biggest competitor in the distributor market

To go direct or not to go direct?

"Going direct" means you publish your book directly on one of the many eretailer sites instead of using a distributor like Smashwords or Draft2Digital. Unless you're a big seller already, you have to go direct to Amazon. For the other sites, you have the choice of either handling each place yourself or using a distributor.

Benefits of going direct

-You can track sales much easier.
-Royalties are generally higher.
-You generally receive your payments 60 days after the end of the month.
-You can update your book much quicker.
-Running short-term discount sales is a lot easier.

Benefits of using a distributor

-You upload your book to one place and you're done.
-The distributor handles all the uploading to other sites.
-To run sales, you change the price in one place and wait for it to trickle to other sites.
-To update your book, you only have to upload it once.

Downsides of going direct
-You have to manage several sites at once.
-To change your book, you have to upload to each and every eretailer individually.

Downsides of using a distributor
-Lower royalty rates
-Payments are generally delayed by quite a bit.
-You have to wait for the retailers to report sales to the distributor before you can look at them.
-Running short-term discounts is very difficult.
-You have to wait for the distributor to send out updated versions of your book to the sites. (Could take weeks sometimes)

Which option do I choose? I go direct to Amazon and Barnes & Noble. Then I use Smashwords for everything else. Why? First, I don't own a Mac, so going direct to iTunes is impossible. Second, I'm a bit lazy, so I much prefer only having to manage a few places instead of a dozen. To me, the benefits outweigh the losses. You will need to weigh all your options and decide what will be best for you.

Using Amazon KDP

The most powerful platform out there today is Amazon. You *must* be on Amazon. Plain and simple. And it really is simple.

- If you don't have an Amazon account already, create one. If you do, you'll just use that. To get to KDP, go to http://kdp.amazon.com.
- Click Add New Title.
- Enter your book details.
- If your book is part of a series, make sure you check the box that says "This book is part of a series" and enter the title and series number.
- Description: Make sure your blurb is catching and hooks the reader. Remember, you don't have to give them a synopsis. They don't need to know everything that's going to happen. You just have to get them to want to read the book.
- Book contributors: If this is your first time publishing, this part might be a bit confusing. Click Add Contributors. Type in your first and last names. Under Title, select Author. You can also add your editor, cover designer, etc in this place if you so choose.
- ISBN: Contrary to popular belief, you *do not* need an ISBN. Amazon assigns one for you.
- Verify your rights: Most of the time, your book will not be public domain. If you wrote the book yourself, it's not public domain.
- Target Categories: Categories are important. You want to choose categories that fit your book well.

- Keywords are just as important as categories, if not more so. This is where you're weedle down those broad categories to get into the smaller niches. This KDP guide is super handy when you're trying to find fitting categories.
- DRM: This is entirely up to you. A quick explanation- If you DRM your book, people can't format it to read on other ereaders. If you don't, they can. There are a bajillion discussions out there about it. Do your research and choose the option best for you.
- Preview your book using the provided viewer. Make sure it looks good and make any changes necessary, then click Save and Continue.
- Rights & Pricing
- Worldwide Rights: Generally, you'll want to choose this. Again, it's that whole eggs in one basket thing. As long as you have the legal right to sell in every country, choose that option. Don't hold your book back from one group of people.
- Royalty: If you're selling your book between 2.99 and 9.99, choose the 70% royalty rate. Set your price and let Amazon populate the rest. You can set each individually if you want, but again, I'm lazy.
- Matchbook: If you have a print version of your book, you can offer the ebook for cheaper or free to anyone who buys it (an awesome perk and incentive to buy both)
- Lending: If you're using the 70% royalty rate, this is already checked. If you're using 35%, you have the option to allow lending. Lending is

kind of lame, really. You can lend the book once to one person for two weeks, and that's it. So it doesn't really hurt anything if you allow lending. I almost always do.

- Terms: You have to check the Terms and Conditions box before you can
- Save and Publish!
- Wait. Usually the wait isn't very long. You can check your Bookshelf regulary to see if the ASIN is up. Once your book has an ASIN, you should be able to go to www.amazon.com/dp/ASIN to buy your book. The book will be available before you receive the email notification from Amazon.

Nook Press and iTunes

Nook Press is Barnes & Noble's e-publishing platform, much like Amazon's KDP platform. Before moving to NookPress, they used PubIt!. Personally, I preferred PubIt! and after they made the switch, I stopped using it and went through Smashwords for most of my books. I left the books I already had direct up there, but any new books I put through Smashwords. For detailed instructions on using NookPress, you can go to https://www.nookpress.com/support/faq.

iTunes is another platform I distribute to through Smashwords. I make quite a few sales over there, but as I don't have a Mac, I can't upload to them directly. There are people out there who will upload for you, but I'm wary about giving my account information to someone else, so I stick to using verified distributors.

Smashwords

Smashwords can be a bit tricky. To initially upload your book, go to www.smashwords.com and click Publish. Once your book is uploaded, though, you'll use the Dashboard to manage everything. Only use Publish to upload *NEW* books.

- Set up your account.
- Click Publish.
- Enter the Title of your book, choose Immediate Release or set up a preorder date, and add the description. The most important description is the Short description.
- Under Pricing, set your price. *Do not* choose Let my readers determine the price, as most eretailers do not allow that.
- Choose the categories (usually the same ones you'll use for Amazon), then add the tags like you did on Amazon.
- Pick which ebook formats to allow (I use all of them).
- Upload your cover and ebook.
- Check YES, I agree and click Publish.

And that's it! You're done.

Createspace Formatting

The Power Players

When you type "print on demand" into a web search, you get back scads of results. Everything you need is on that first page, though. The top players in the POD game are Lulu, Lightning Source, and Createspace. There are several others that get mentioned, such as Bookbaby and Cafepress, but Lulu, Lightning Source, and Createspace are definitely the biggest fish in the pond at this time.

A VERY quick run-down of the big three

I prefer Createspace (reasons why in a moment), but there are some things to note about the others.

Lulu is similar to Createspace in many aspects, though they don't offer as much for royalty through Amazon. They do, however, offer hardcover books that are very easy to order.

Lightning Source charges you to upload initially, where the other two companies only take royalties.

Why Createspace?

The short answer is: It was the easiest to use when I was starting out. I started using Createspace back in 2011. Since then, I have published seven books with them, soon to be nine. Why?

1) They're easy to use. They have a very simple layout and make it super easy to upload.

2) They're directly connected to Amazon, and since Amazon is the biggest bookseller, it makes sense to use a company that will let you get the best royalty rates through them.

3) It's the one I've been using since the start, so I'm comfortable with them and familiar with the process.

4) Despite popular belief, they *do* actually have the capability to print hardcover books. Most people say they don't, but they do. You just have to ask.

Don't take my word for it, though. Before you commit to a print-on-demand publisher, do your research. Decide which one will be the best for you, and check them all out. And if you try one and don't like it, you can always give another POD a shot on your next book.

Style Sheets

You could do what I did for my first several books and download the templates from Createspace to use for creating your print book. But if you do, you might also do the same thing I did and screw up the formatting on those templates, repeatedly, and beat your head against the computer trying to fix it, for hours on end until you wanted to curl up in bed and cry yourself to sleep. I used to be terrified of style sheets. They were these beasts that I knew nothing about. They were cryptic and sounded way too complicated. But fighting with the templates took *hours of my life* and in the end, I realized how simple it was to create my book using style sheets. Now I can knock out formatting in an hour on the shorter pieces. Easy peasy.

So the first thing we want to do before we start formatting at all is *Save our file.* Do a SAVE AS and save your novel so you don't mess up your original file. I generally use the same file I used to format the ebook, so I save it as *bookname_CS.*

Once you have it saved, you're ready to start playing.

Quick note: I use OpenOffice, so all my terminology is for that. Word has similar options, so all of this information should work fine there, you may just have to do a tiny bit of searching to find what you're looking for.

Creating the style sheets

I generally only use two styles-- Default and First Page. If you have downloaded a Createspace template, you'll end up with a bajillion and one style sheets, but you only really need the two to do simple formatting.

There are three ways to get to the Styles page. The easiest is to hit F11. The second easiest is to click that little button on the left-hand side of the screen that looks like a piece of paper with a volume bar on it. If neither of those work, you can go to *Format->Styles and Formatting*. Once that box pops up, click on *Page Styles* (the second button from the right).

Default

To change the page size, *right-click* on Default and choose *Modify*. Under *Page*, set your Width and Height. The two most common are 5x8 and 6x9. (*Note: If you have a cover already created, make sure you pick the size that fits with your cover.*) Orientation is typically going to be Portrait, unless you're getting really fancy schmancy, which I never do. Under Layout Settings->Page Layout, choose Mirrored and Format is 1, 2, 3.

You generally have a little wiggle room with your margins. If you're comfortable playing around with them, feel free. Createspace requires a *minimum* Inner margin of 0.75". I generally use 0.90", as it gives a bit more white space on the inside and works for almost any book size. Smaller margins will allow more words to be on the page and decrease your page count. Larger margins add more white space and look a little nicer (entirely my opinion, of course). Test them out and see what looks best to you.

On that same screen, you'll see Header and Footer. Click on Header. If you want your name and the title of your book at the top of the pages*, check the box for Header On. *Deselect* Same content left/right. The margins are again adjustable, so choose what looks best to you. I typically leave Left and Right at 0, Spacing at 0.20" and Height at 0.04". I also check Use dynamic spacing and Autofit height.

Here's an example of a page layout:

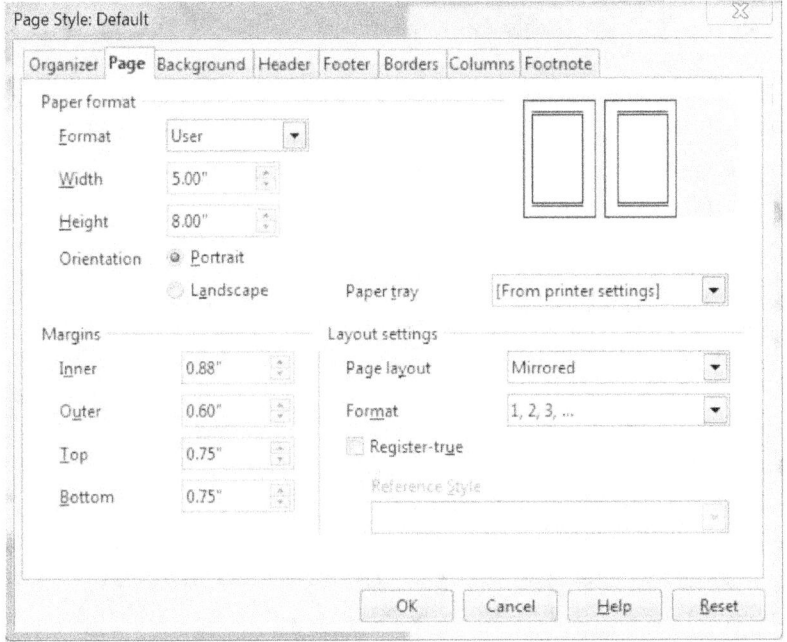

Under Footer, check Footer on *and* Same content left/right, as you want the numbers to scale properly on both sides. The margins are the same as the ones for Header.

Once those are done, click OK.

First Page

Now we're going to do the same for First Page. *Right-click* First Page and choose Modify. Under Organizer, set Next Style to First Page. We're using First Page instead of Default so we don't have to manually add breaks to each page we want a blank header/footer on.

Under Page, set everything as you did for Default. You want them to be exactly the same. If they're not, the book won't line up properly and Createspace will yell at you. We don't like being yelled at.

Now here's where things really differ. Under both Header and Footer, *uncheck* Header on and Footer on. You don't want a header or footer on any of the pages we'll use First Page for.

Click OK and you're good to go.

Other

Now we want to set up a style sheet for the random page we might encounter where want don't want a header or footer, but we don't want to have to redo all the pages after that particular page, either. Right-click on Default and then New. Name your new style whatever you want. I usually leave it at Untitled1 or set it to Other. Set the Next Style to Default. Make the Page settings *exactly* like you did for Default and First Page, then *uncheck* the boxes on Header and Footer.

*Note: If you're doing a non-fiction book and want each chapter to have a different header at the top of the page, you will need to set up styles for each and every chapter.

And that's it for your Style Sheets. Onto the formatting!

Front Matter

What is front matter?

Front matter is all that mumbo jumbo that fills up the pages before the story actually starts. In some books, there will be a lot of front matter. In most fiction books, all you'll really have are:
Title page
Copyright page
Maybe a dedication page

In non-fiction, you could have things like:
Preface page
Acknowledgements page
Table of contents
Notes
Random pages added in just because you can

Title Page

The title page is super simple. You'll want your title centered on the page in big, bold letters and you'll want your name below that, a little smaller, but still bold. Like so.

Queen of Hearts

Book 2 of
The Risen King

Samantha Warren

To make sure you don't end up with headers or page numbers, open your style sheet box (F11) and double-click on First Page.

Copyright Page

The copyright page is super simple. Keep in clean and only include the necessary information. To add a break between the title and copyright page, go to Insert-> Manual Break -> Page Break. Feel free to borrow the copyright info below.

The Body

Page Numbers

Now onto the most important part: The Body. This is the part where we want to use page numbers, so click just before Chapter 1, go to Insert->Manual Break. Choose Page Break. Under Style, select Default. Check the box that says Change page number, and set the number to 1. That will make Chapter 1 start on page 1. Neat, huh?

At this point, you probably don't have page numbers, either. Let's fix that. On the first page of Chapter 1, click on the very bottom of the page in the white space. You should see a cursor pop up. Up under Insert again, choose Fields, then Page Number. You should see a little 1 pop up. I like to center my page numbers, but you can set them wherever you want to put them. You can even add nifty little brackets around them, like so: [1] or ~1~. Just remember that whatever you put on the first page will follow through the rest of the book.

Headers

If you chose to have headers, click at the top of the page and add them in. Generally, the title will go on the left page and the author name on the right, but as with everything, it's your book, your choice.

Chapter Headings

Everyone wants their chapter titles to look nice. Some want them simple, some want them really fancy, but we all want them nice. You can do a couple things here. You can use the fonts you have, you can buy new fonts, or you can use an image. With the images, keep them small, keep them neat, and make sure they are a minimum of 300 dpi. Whatever you do, keep it consistent throughout the book, from the spaces between the top and text to the centering. Clean and professional is the way to go.

Body Text

It's important to not get too fancy with the body of the chapters. The best way to check if you have things set up correctly is to highlight a couple paragraphs, right-click, and choose Paragraph. I like to set my Indents & Spacing like this:

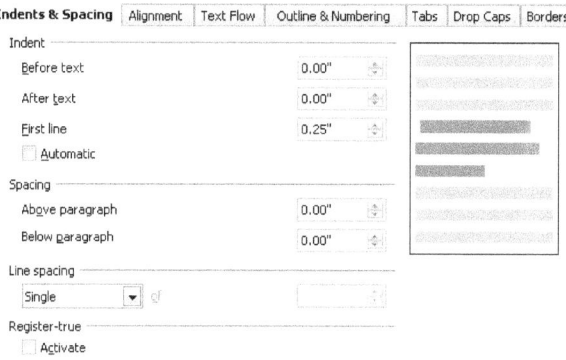

The other thing you want to do on this screen is go to the Alignment tab and set the alignment to Justified. If you open any print book and look inside, you'll see that the right side and left side both line up nicely along the margins. Setting your text to Justified will do this. You don't want to leave it all scraggly and uneven. Neat and sweet is what we need.

Orphans and Widows

These are terms that are often used in traditional publishing. According to Wiki:

Orphan: A paragraph-opening line that appears at the bottom of a page, or a word, part of a word, or very short line that appears by itself at the end of a paragraph, resulting in too much whitespace.

Widow: A paragraph-ending line that falls at the beginning of the following page, thus separated from the rest of the text.

You don't have to worry about these with ebooks because the e-retailers take care of them when they convert your book. Not so much with print. You have to deal with these yourself. Like usual, you have options with that. The first, and easiest, is to go to the same place we were with the Indents & Spacing and Alignment. You'll see the Text Flow tab.

The first thing to do here (no matter which route you choose) is to uncheck Hyphenation. You don't want any weird hyphenation issues in your book. If you find words that do need to be hyphenated, do it yourself. For the orphans and widows, check Orphan Control and Widow Control. Set both to 2 lines. If you select 3 lines, there will be too much white space at the bottom of a page, and 1 line defeats the purpose.

You can also do what I do and handle the widows and orphans yourself. Uncheck everything on the Text Flow page before you do this. I find that doing it myself leaves less white space at the bottom of the pages and leads to an overall cleaner feel. Plus, I'm a self-publisher. I like to have as much control over my formatting as possible.

Back Matter

Back matter is all the stuff that falls after the story is over. I usually include just a few things:

A note that says something along the lines of "Thank you for reading. If you enjoyed this book, please consider leaving a review. For more from this author, please sign up for the newsletter."

A list of other books I've published so if they really enjoyed the book, they can go buy more.

An About the Author page with a short bio and contact information

Note: Remember to put full links in if you use them anywhere. A print book is not clickable!

The back matter is the last thing a person sees, so make it good. But you also want to make it short and sweet. As a wise man named Hugh Howey once said, you don't want to detract from the feeling of your book. Make sure your back matter doesn't take away from what they've just read. Let them remember it. Let them revel in it.

You don't have to do anything special for the back matter, either, as far as style sheets go. It can keep the same style as the main body. Use the same format for your headings here as you did in your chapters, as well.

And that's it. Do a couple more checks through your book to make sure it looks good, and then that's it. You're ready to print!

Publishing Your Print Book

You've followed all the steps up to this point, you have your file ready to go, and you want to upload to Createspace, right? The first thing you need to do is create an account, if you haven't already. So go ahead and do that. Done? Good. Now we need to set up the book.

Add Project

Click the button that says Add Project. The first page you will see lets you enter your book's title. Make sure you use proper capitalization and such, as this is what will show on Amazon. After you've done that, choose Paperback in the next box, then select Guided Process. Once you're comfortable with publishing, you can use the Expert, but for now, let Createspace help you out.

Title Information

Most of this page is self-explanatory. Enter the title, your name (or if you're publishing for someone else, their name), if it's in a series, etc. See? It's easy so far, right? Click Save & Continue and let's move onto the next step, which is a super important step.

ISBN

You cannot publish a print book without an ISBN, plain and simple. But you have many options on how to get one. You can buy one. This can be extremely expensive, though. Or you can let Createspace help you out. I usually choose the Free option, as I don't sell my books through bookstores. My print copies are mainly for special purposes and the free option is fine. Look at all of them and decide which option is best for you. Once you've figured it out, select it, fill out any other information it requests, and hit Assign.

Note: Now that you have your ISBN, you need to head back to your file and enter it on the copyright page just under the copyright info. Once you've done that, save the file, then go to File and Export as PDF. Make sure you choose the options for PDF/A 1-a and Export automatically inserted blank pages. Once you've done that, you're ready to move onto the next step.

Trim Size

Trim size is how big your book is going to be. Make sure you choose the same size you chose when you were setting up your file. They *must* match.

Also on this page, you'll find where you set the interior color (in most cases, you're going to stick to Black & White), and the color of the paper. White is a very bright white and cream is an off-white or sometimes tan color. As with everything else, choose the color that fits best with your aesthetic. Some covers work better with white paper, some work better with cream. If you don't like it the first time, you can always change it. No biggie.

Then upload your file, and click Save.

Cover

I highly suggest you get your cover professionally done. The first thing anyone sees it the cover, so you want it to really hit them and make them check out your book. No matter what, you'll select whether you want Matte or Glossy. Again, this will be based on your cover. Some covers, like my zombie western, look best in matte, and some, like my paranormal romance, look best in glossy.

If you have someone do your cover for you, you'll skip straight to the Upload a Print-Ready PDF and follow the instructions. If you have your own, or only have the front cover or a jpg, you can build your cover online using their easy-peasy cover creator. You can also hire Createspace to create a cover for you.

Review

Once everything is set up, you can submit your book for review. While you're waiting for the review to go through, set up your price, distribution channels, and description. Again, choose the options that will best help you meet your goals. Createspace has some very good information in each section, so make sure you read them thoroughly if you have any questions at all.

Proof

You've got everything set up, dealt with any issues Createspace brought up during the review, and now it's time to proof. For your first several copies, it's an extremely good idea to order the copies so you can physically hold them in your hands. The online reviewer is nice and I use it often, but if you're not familiar with how a proof copy should look, do yourself a favor and order a copy. Plus, there's nothing like that feeling of seeing your book in print for the first time, and this is your first chance to do that.

Approve That Baby!

If you've looked through the proof and decided it looks great, if you have everything set up correctly, it's time to take the big leap. Approve your book!

Now you can order copies for friends, family, and fans. It'll also be available for purchase on places like Amazon, and if you chose the Expanded Distribution, other bookstores can order as well. And that's it. You're done. Time to start writing the next book.

Happy Publishing!

Thank you!

Thank you for reading *The Quick & Dirty Guide Series.* If you enjoyed the book, please take a moment to review it on your favorite ebook retailer's website or share with your friends.

For a little peek into the craziness that is my writer life, please sign up for my email list.
http://www.samantha-warren.com/updates

Other Books

Battle of Black River
Blood of the Dragon
Winds from the North

Vampire Assassin (Jane #1)
New Blood (Jane #2)
Blood & Tears (Jane #3)
Redemption (Jane #4)
Til Death (Jane #5)
Blood Moon (Jane #6)
A Magical Christmas (Jane #6.5)
Cursed (Jane #7)
Witchfire (Jane #8)
Bloodfeud (Jane #9)
Bloodshed (Jane #10)

The Seven Keys of Alaesha

Massacre at Lonesome Ridge
Blood & Dust

The Iron Locket (The Risen King #1)
Sir Kay and the White Lady (A TRK Short)
Queen of Hearts (TRK #2)
Night Terrors (A TRK Novella)
The Risen King (TRK #3)

About the Author

Samantha Warren is a fantasy and science fiction author who spends her days immersed in dragons, spaceships, and vampires. With her pet dragon, Anethesis, she ventured to the ends of the universe, but the cost of space travel cut into her sock fetish fund, so she sold her ship and returned home. She milks cows for fun, collects zombie gnomes, and spends a lot of time in her weed patch (aka: garden), watching any show featuring Gordon Ramsay, or posting random things on her blog.

Send me a message!
Email: samantha@samantha-warren.com
Twitter: @_SamanthaWarren
Blog: http://www.samantha-warren.com
Facebook: http://www.facebook.com/AuthorSamanthaWarren